ZONDERkidz | I Can Read! | SHARED My First READING

The Beginner's Bible®

Adam and Eve in the Garden

D0179865

pictures by Kelly Pulley

In the beginning,
the world was empty.
But God had a plan.

"I will make
many good things,"
God said.

On day one God said,
"I will make day and night."
So he did.

On day two God split
the water from the air.
He said, "Here are the sky
and the sea."

God made land on day three.

Plants grew on the land.

Fruit trees grew there, too.

On day four God put the sun
and the moon in the sky.

On day five
God made birds
to fly in the sky.

He made fish to swim
in the ocean.

Day six was busy, too.
God made the rest
of the animals.

Then God made the first man.

God named him Adam.

God loved Adam.

God rested on day seven.

He was so happy!

Adam was happy, too.

God put Adam in a garden.

The garden was called Eden.

Adam took care of Eden.

He took care of the animals.

He even named all the animals. "You will be called a 'parrot.' You will be called a 'butterfly.'"

One day God made Eve.
She helped Adam take care of
the garden and the animals.

God gave Adam and Eve one rule.
God said, "Do not eat
fruit from this tree."

Later, a sneaky snake
was in the tree.

"Eve, you can eat this fruit.
It is fine!" the snake said.

Eve ate the fruit.

Then Adam ate the fruit, too.

God was sad.

They had broken his one rule.

This was called a "sin."

"Eve gave me the fruit,"
Adam said.

"Snake tricked me," Eve said.

God said, "Snake,
you must move on your
belly and eat dust."

God told Adam and Eve,
"You must leave.
You did not follow my rule."

Adam and Eve left the garden.
They were very sad.

But God would always love them.

He made another plan.

One day, God would send Jesus. Jesus would save everyone from their sins.